The New Pornography

The New Pornography
Patrick Chapman

Published in 1996 by
Salmon Publishing Ltd,
Knockeven, Cliffs of Moher,
Co. Clare.

© Patrick Chapman 1996.

The moral right of the author has been asserted.

A catalogue record for this book is available
from the British Library.

Salmon Publishing acknowledges the support of the Arts Council.

ISBN 1 897648 77 4

All rights reserved. No part of this publication may be reproduced or transmitted in any form or by any means, electronic or mechanical, including photography, recording, or any information storage or retrieval system, without permission in writing from the publisher. The book is sold subject to the condition that it shall not, by way of trade or otherwise, be lent, resold or otherwise circulated without the publisher's prior consent in any form of binding or cover other than that in which it is published and without a similar condition, including this condition, being imposed on the subsequent purchaser.

Cover design by Estresso.
Set in Janson.
Printed by Colour Books,
Baldoyle Ind. Est., Dublin 13.

The New Pornography

Eavan Boland, writing in *Poetry Ireland Review*, praised Patrick Chapman's 'real gifts for rhythmic shock treatment and off-beat diction,' describing him as 'one of the very compelling voices' of the new generation of Irish poets.

Chapman's first book of poems, *Jazztown* (Raven, 1991), was hailed as 'a remarkably confident, not to say swaggering, debut for a poet still in his early twenties' by *The Irish Times*.

Books Ireland said: 'A sharp and startling debut it surely is. His urban vignettes, while appearing relaxed, are honed down till every word pays its way.'

The Steeple poetry magazine welcomed it as a 'First collection by a young writer who refuses to play safe. Wonderful, original, modern fables are encountered in this book. One of the few books around which is compelling to read.'

Chapman's work has appeared widely in periodicals and was featured in the anthology *Real Cool: Poems To Grow Up With* (Marino, 1995).

He was shortlisted for an Ian St James Award in 1990, and a Sunday Tribune Hennessy Award for poetry in 1989 and 1995.

Patrick Chapman was born in August 1968 and lives in Dublin where he works as a copywriter.

By the same author

Jazztown

Acknowledgements

The Black Pool, Copacetic, Cyphers, Envoi, Poetry Ireland Review, RTE, The Steeple, Undr, Windows.

An Arts Council Artflight Travel Award in 1991 is gratefully acknowledged.

Special thanks to Caitriona Chapman who set some of these poems to music.

To Kieran.

Contents

United States

Night on 109th Street	3
Status Symbols	5
An Eye in Central Park	6
Campin's *Triptych of the Annunciation*	7
New York Food Chain	8
A Neat Idea	9
San Andreas Fault	10
Keraunothetophobia	11
A Dream of Space Flight	12
Nantahala Falls	13
Break Up	14
Shoe Shine in New Orleans	15
Montezuma Fish	16

Necropolis Chic

All Flesh is Grasmere	19
Pastoral Hiss	20
Necropolis Chic	22
Prayer of the Projectile	23
Extraterrestrials	24
Concentration	25

Blind Voyeur

Advice to Intending Visitors	31
In the Old Town Square	32
The Communist	33
Return of the Golem	34
The Hunchback and the Concave-Bellied Dwarf	35

The New Pornography

Backward Child	41
The New Pornography I	43
The New Pornography II	44
The New Pornography III	45
Jocasta Tree	46
Lunatic Dream	47
Dead Zone	48
X^2	49
Vibrating Love Nest	50
Weekend	51
In Every Dream Home	52
Lipstick Blood	53
Nuclear Love Poem	55

Disease Variations

I am John's Virus	61
Vitreous China	62
Short-Love Couplets	63
Viral	64
In Extremis	65
Sympathy	66
Sub Rosa	67
Robert Mapplethorpe	68

United States

Night on 109th Street

Forbidden to smoke in the apartment,
I sit up on the roof and watch the trails of passing aeroplanes
And automobile streams of red and brilliant white on Broadway.

I can hear the car alarms set off by landing firecrackers;
See the fire hydrant spray an arc across the street.

I spy on Pedro Gomez doing business on the stoop with neighbours,
Drinking muddy beer infused with cheap tabasco sauce.
Sometimes he will piss between the buildings.

By De Los Santos travel shop beside La Ronda bar,
A Mustang, live with light, pumps hot merengue
While the driver ~ buying beers in L'Español off-licence take away ~
Is asking Pedro's daughter: 'Baby, how much for a suck?'

From an open third floor window comes a sudden creak of cello;
From another, further down, I hear a football game in Spanish.

A man in an adjacent building ~ cooking supper in the nude ~
Will later masturbate into his window box nasturtiums.

In a taller building opposite a woman puts to bed a
  child
In front of whom, this evening, I have seen her making
  love.

After I have smoked enough I walk towards the stairs
And climb across the wall by which someone from
  down below
Found me asleep this morning, in the sunshine, getting
  burnt.

Status Symbols

On Broadway and West 109
I see a Spanish American
Who boasts a pillar of air
Where his leg stops at the knee.

He seems to have taken
A shine to those crutches.

As luck would have it, then,
I spot another man
Whose left shoe sole
~ Four inches taller than his right ~
Supports a leg truncated at the shin.

Those who can afford them wear prosthetics:

In a bar where there were posters
Advertising late night music
I enquired of one such man
If he intended to go dancing.

An Eye in Central Park

Last night, between
the Summerstage and wall,
I found an eye.

Its rods and cones inert,
the eye was caked in sand
and trailing nerve tissue.

Operational,
it might have witnessed
jogging, wilding, rollerblading,

Shakespeare in the Park
or vagabonds evicted
from Strawberry Fields.

I picked it up.
It had definitely been
a human eye.

In my hand the membrane burst
and humour greased my palm
so I put it in my pocket

wondering if the final image
captured on the retina
was of a plucking finger.

Campin's *Triptych of the Annunciation*

Cloisters Museum, 1991

On the table beside her, a candle goes out.
Mary is reading a cloth-bound edition
of Margaret Mitchell's *Gone With The Wind*
especially imported from the future.

An angel has arrived to tell her
of her imminent ear infection:
airborne baby Jesus,
naked as the day he will be born,
is going to crash into her cochlea
and she knows nothing about it.

Why the ear?

Mediaeval man could not consider
penetration in the usual place,
preferring this exoticism.

Neither could he countenance
the concept of pre-natal classes,
Spock or yoga, let alone
maternity leave
or ear-muff contraception.

New York Food Chain

'In the future, no-one will go hungry.
The underclasses will be catered for ~
fed on blood to make their pelts shine,
then served with sauce and garnish
in the fashionable restaurants.

'West side immigrants ~ who'll dine
on shrink-wrapped meningitic brains
available on offer at the superstores ~
will have their fifteen minutes
on the place-mats of suburbanites.'

A Neat Idea

In the more upmarket
Manhattan bars,
patrons can join
the mile high club
without a plane:

Installed in the rest rooms are found
condominium vending machines.

You can pick someone up,
then buy the apartment
to take him back to.

San Andreas Fault

'I live on the fault line,'
whispers Anabel into her dictaphone.

She frets that when tectonic plates
make quakes in California
and it crumbles into the Pacific ~
America, distracted, will not notic
e.

Keraunothetophobia[1]

In memoriam, Mars Observer

Skylab set me going.

In nineteen seventy nine
I began to wear a hard hat
even in the shower,
should a sliver of antenna
punch a hole through our ceiling.

Nineteen eighty-six was bad:
the Challenger exploded.
I double glazed our windows
and I camouflaged the roof
to make it look like grass.

Still, no tail fin, fuselage or wing
collided with my head.
I added padding to the hard hat.

Now I wait for Alpha,
Giotto, Pioneer and Hubble; I
wait for my Newton's apple.

---

[1] Fear of being struck by returning satellite debris.

A Dream of Space Flight

At the Air and Space Museum, alone,
Vacationing in Washington,
I look down from the body
Of the never-to-be-space-flown Sky
Lab sister ship at Sally Ride in mannequin.

*

Since Columbia first hit the sky,
My only ambition has been
To look from on high at the land
Where, in the fifties, my husband
Had built his own radio station;
To marvel a while at Long Island
Where first I had fallen in love;
To see the Earth once from above
Before I die.

Nantahala Falls

For Kim, Orla and Michael

We rafted seven miles along the Nantahala river.
Often, we would pull into a bank to bale out water.
One such time, a snake stunned Kim in fear.

I was thrown at Nantahala Falls, the final rapid.
Caught between the rubber and the rock,
I clawed above the surface then slipped back ~
Ready to let water make me cork.
I clawed again and found the cord;
Michael and Orla pulled me aboard.

We landed on the bank where buses waited;
Dragged the raft ashore, upturned it;
Banged life jackets on the gravel; chatted
About reptiles, chiggers, oars and drowning, rapids.

I sat on a rock and, shaking water from a shoe,
Recalled the anaesthetic Nantahala, coming to.

Break Up

In Marie Laveau's, a witch has made a spell
With alligator tooth and powdered snail shell:

You will leave me for a woman you can love.

Later, in a Mississippi market
~ Arcade cornucopia of flower, anther, stamen, shoot ~
We pass a cardboard sign above a still unpurchased cot:

'Pregnant, or just thinking about it?'

I distract you with enamel earrings (blue):
I, not you, will leave and when I do,
I'll sleep with any gin-dead stranger who
Will have me and my crazy love for you.

Shoe Shine in New Orleans

'I bet a dollar I can tell you
Where you got those shoes.'

I ask where. He tells me:
'Right there on your feet!'

I give him a dollar. He offers a shine
Then brags of when the rains come

Bringing cockroaches the size of rats
And rats the size of motorbikes.

'I know which year you finished school.'

'Senior year,' I answer. He:
'For that, your shoe shine is for free.'

Then he bends over backwards
To look in the shine
With the eyes in the back of his head.

Montezuma Fish

River through the jungle:
    Fish wait for conquistador
        Stopping for a call of nature,

Urinating in the water.

Fish sense uric acid, jump
    And ride the yellow waterfall ~
        Spines flick into flesh like fishing hooks.

Necropolis Chic

(1992)

All Flesh is Grasmere

In a pub in Grasmere I recall
The ghosts around Dove Cottage.
De Quincey: an opium billow unfurling;
The drinkers: a phantasmagorical brawl;
Leaving the spirit of Wordsworth: an image
Trapped in a painting, forever dictating.

Pastoral Hiss

Squashed pellets of sheep dung:
Like the heads of tiny drumsticks on my shoes.
I beat a tattoo to the estuary.

Barbed wire on ditches quivers,
Threatening the composition
Of my grass-contaminated clothes.

Offsetting this greenery,
Ahead, is Heysham nuclear power station.

Squinting, I see clouds retreat from it
Reluctant to be drawn in and arranged
Along the pylons' wires whose hum
Forms a setting for the counterpoint
Of cars on unseen roads.

Sheep go crazy here,
The signals in their neurons
Re-orchestrated by loose ions.

Humans, schizophrenic in proximity
~ Their brains re-scored and dissonant ~
Eat the crazy sheep and drink irradiated water.

Eventually they'll die like the dogs who, alive,
Are deranged here and tethered to gates,
Barking at bum notes like me.

To find my place, I'd need a Geiger counter ~
Brandishing it like a baton
In the coughing air of Heysham,
Conducting atomic concertos,
Atonal.

Necropolis Chic

Half a house is beautiful and quiet in conceit,
Aware that every passing brickie
Whistles at its open door.

Its neighbour is a Catholic house
~ A two up and two down ~
But bricked and boarded.

Demolition makes a catwalk of the city:
Draped in rubble, houses are on show
For how much bomb it took to make them.

Prayer of the Projectile

Born as you were born, through a passage,
But mine, a metal birth canal:
I am the bullet that kills you.

Hammer strike like the shock
That may kick-start your heart in hospital;
The smoke and shell: my afterbirth;
That bang: all labour pangs in one:
I am the bullet that kills you.

The one who pulls the trigger now recoils.
The stock against the shoulder smarts.

I hit without a ricochet,
Trajectory unwavering.

I am the bullet that kills you.

Extraterrestrials

The reflected clouds I saw from Albert Bridge
Appeared to float on the Lagan
Like boat-planes from another planet.

On the road to Dublin I passed pylons
Massed inside a compound,
Their lights remote: a star field
Through which ETs have arrived.

You find their effects in the landscape.
I took with me a shard of stained glass window:
A fragment of the Crown bar
Made forensic by a car bomb.

Concentration

Train

The carriage doors shut
On nude bodies
Hanging on railings,
Communicating
By scent:

Between my skin and your olfactories,
Pheromones alert you to my presence.

Now the train is overground:
A shuttling procession. Every
Window's daylight is an oven door.

A Dream

We were fed on our own flesh.

Once I ate the arm of a postman,
Imagining the information
Carried by the tip of my food,
The secrets known to my supper.

Vertical Horizon

While crouching in the dark I spied,
Through Eiffel Tower-tall wire fence,
An Arianespace rocket
Captured like an after-image
On a roll of film.

First frame: nose cone;
Last frame: thruster.

Soon there was no sky.

The rocket passed
Through dislocating
Loci.

Zero

Taken to a field of rubble
Contours bounding furrow graves
Ploughed open by our forebears,

    We are frames:

Skin suspended from skeletal rack;
Pelvic bone, collar, kneecap protruding.

    Each executing, in turn,
    The inmate in front
    With a hammer,

We domino into the earth in a row
That's as neat as we're able to make it.

Blind Voyeur

Advice to Intending Visitors

By the river is a plaque for Jan Palach.
You will pass it on the way to Charles Bridge.
Please take a photograph for reference
And think no more about it until,
Reading in *Prognosis* of the imminent divorce,
Consider pouring petrol on your map and lighting it:
    For Palach's immolation, Havel's velvet revolution.

(1992)

In the Old Town Square

In a bar in Staré mésto
I wrote you a postcard.

The obverse: a picture
of the old Jewish cemetery.

The reverse, in ballpoint,
read: *Wish you were here.*

The Communist

I am buying dated atlases ~ drawn up
Before a port wine stain became our map ~
To stack them, thousands tall,
Like bricks in some new Berlin Wall.

Return of the Golem

He will form again from darkness
in a sealed room in a synagogue
somewhere in the Jewish quarter.

In this post-superstitious age
how will he make a living?

He could guest on talk shows:

    'Was Gustav Meyrink lying?
    'What of Wegener's three films?
    'Why were you not at Terezín?'

The Hunchback and the
Concave-Bellied Dwarf

i

A convex hammock
On which I mould my body asleep,
It is a comfort to me ~
The hump upon the hunchback's back.

I wrap my legs around his neck.
I hook my thumbs in his belt loops.
I sleep until the moon makes water
Well up in that water bed of skin.

When, under my weight, it bursts,
I wake.

ii

She spends her mornings
Putting poultice on the hump
Until it heals.

By noon, the skin and gristle's knitted smooth:
This dome on which she sleeps.

iii

He breaks my nose on Saturdays;
Sundays, breaks my spine.
By Monday I am well again;
We watch television.

iv

I take her belt with one hand
And her collar with the other
Then fling her through the dust
That, through the skylight,
Pins the room down.

The New Pornography

'It's an interesting question: in what way is intercourse per vagina more stimulating than with this ashtray, say, or with the angle between two walls? Sex is now a conceptual act, it's probably only in terms of the perversions that we can make contact with each other at all...'

~ J.G. Ballard
The Atrocity Exhibition

Backward Child

Back before senses,
A knot of flesh unties,
An incision is unmade.

Waters, unbroken again, swirl.
I curl and close my eyes, an embryo.

Placenta reattached and agony annulled,
Lips press closed.

My heart rewinds,
Brain becomes ganglia.
I am a zygote.

*Elsewhere, baby clothes rewrap, unwrap again
And find themselves back in the shop.*

A speck lodged in the lining of the uterus, then loose,
I am gametes at point of contact, separating.
Suddenly, the ovum hits fallopian;
Spermatozoa hightail back to vulva
Where a penis is withdrawing.

They coalesce into a milk
That nestles back inside the testicles;
Ovum finds an ovary and sleeps.

The woman on the bed is cooling.
Arched, she untears panties off her hips;
Her stomach muscles tight, her belly flat.

The man is buttoning and off the boil.
He says 'I love you' in reverse
And, backwards, leaves the room.

The woman, whom he'd woken, dreams
That soon he will arrive in here
To interrupt her sleep.

When the night grows back into the day
Through evening, afternoon and morning
~ This night in which I have been unconceived ~
The man and woman have not even met.

(October 1990)

The New Pornography I:
Herschel on Mimas

Put on your dirty grey lab coat.
Take out, extend, your telescope.

Now, look at Herschel, a crater on Mimas,
Orbiting Saturn, hanging alone.

Imagine Herschel as an areola.
Ask:

Could someone cosmological
Lick sensation through a nerve?

Then, before you wash your hands,
Consider someone later feeling

~ Fingers shaped like astronauts ~
For lumps.

The New Pornography II:
Langue d'Amour

Administer the training stimuli.

Your patient will respond
To the application of heat
By sustaining a thermal injury
And to aversive electrical stimulation
By displaying the startle reflex.

Implant a tumour into his throat;
It may encroach on his breathing area.

Introduce tissue into the larynx;
It could cause airway embarrassment.

Sew his eyelids together;
He will experience binocular deprivation.

Crush his cranium;
He will exhibit lethal behaviour.

Now, return to your domicile
And, with your mate, participate
In trim co-ordination.

The New Pornography III:
Tears of the Lonely

i

She does not dream of *Playgirl*
But a pot-pourri of strangers:

Bottom, nipple, vulva, penis,
Whiff of rectum, breast milk, come,
Brown hairy chest, broad back, good chin.

ii

While she compared the feeling to:
Sensation of a million eels
Flagellating toward my head
Upon my intravenous tide...

He'd been thinking of transmitters ~
Message tapped in by her fingers
On the key pad of her clitoris:
Release endorphins; lubricate my lips.

Jocasta Tree

One day, the boy stood beside her
and hugged her as roughly
as twelve year old arms would allow.

Then he let her pierce him with a branch.

Her sap commingled with his blood until
~ ecstatic with her juice in him ~
he began to resemble her.

In dreams on rainy days, he grew bark breasts.
Awake, his elbows and his knees
adopted timber-carapace.

His toes became roots:
cambium-nacre probing for moisture
osmotically introduced
into his lymphatic system.

His arms became branches wrapped around her.

When the first wisps of puberty
happened to him,
she took him inside her and he died.

Lunatic Dream

The scent of cat fur fills the room.
The plop of water dripping from
the south pole of a light bulb
whose filament is amber
meets a storm on television:
Dorothy and Toto have left Kansas.

The pipe between the ceiling
and the floor above has burst
and I am naked, ankle deep
and half-demented in the bath-tub
filled with water boiled in pots
that have been put on, taken off again
a hundred times, it seems.

On my face there is a scratch
that I have put there with a wire brush
with which I now make blood canals
between my shoulder blades

and in my other hand there is the cat:
its fur removed and on the floor,
its claws clipped down to cuticles,
its whiskers all yanked out.

Dead Zone

On the spit of my rejection,
turning on the fire of memory:
the body of a lover, barbecued.

Her muscles wasting; her pulmonary
organ in which blood is pudding;
her arteries and veins, their valves

clogged up, preventing nothing now;
her ligaments and hamstrings
and her tendinitis-loving limbs ~

all separated, all unglued
and all protesting in a hiss:
do not consume what you no longer need.

X^2

A syringe: as much my lover now
as you who had quipped
that should my skin bear stretch marks
you would teach me about stitches;
you who, in denying termination, empathised.

No need now: our tinyhead is here.
I have fulfilled my contractual obligations.

Vibrating Love Nest

Most nights, half an hour
after you have rolled away,
you ask if I'm all right.

I say:
'Uh-huh...'

But not tonight.

*

Tonight you have gone out
to drink some woman pretty;
left me to my own devices:

spotted dick
vibrating love egg
silver lady finger

Weekend

Married for the minute that it takes to get our room
 key
~ It will burn my tongue and yours ~
We'll leave saliva in the keyhole for their eyes.

In Every Dream Home

The last remaining guest is on the carpet.
In her hair our cat will, by the dawn, have given birth.

I throw a wine carafe. You catch it,
Spilling Pinot Noir. I whisper:

'Drink it and come here.
We will make love on the table top
If I can get the drop leaves up.'

In swallows measured breath-like
By the bobbing of the cork, you drink
As though you are in competition.

Then, the bottle empty,
Crumbs of cork around your tongue,
You mumble: 'Get away from me.'

Lipstick Blood

Tonight I found your farewell note
In lipstick, pink, on waxy paper,
Wrapping toblerone.

You had left it on my doorstep
Like a baby in a basket.

*

Earlier, you'd plotted with that lipstick on my chest
An anatomically accurate
Diagram of your heart:

~ Auricle
    (atrium),
        ventricle,
            pacemaker,
                vena cava
                    and aorta.

*

You had said that ~

    ~ Your systole-diastole's a murmur.

    ~ A lifespan is measured by number of beats
      (A cow has the same as a pig or a human).

    ~ If I ever touch you emotionally

    You will break my neck
    With your bare thighs.

Nuclear Love Poem

i

Atoms of our days.

We tender to each other
Albumen of chicken egg

Back and forth
From throat to throat,

The broken surface tension
Of the yolk between our chins.

ii

When we are asleep I suck
The core out of a white dwarf
And give one hemisphere to you.

We pass the halo gas from lung to lung
Until we are one moment of cold fusion.

Disease Variations

'But then, he tells me that everything is erotic, that everything is sexual. You know what I mean? He tells me that even old flesh is erotic flesh, that disease is the love of two alien kinds of creatures for each other, that dying is an act of eroticism.'

~ David Cronenberg
Shivers

I am John's Virus

I painted purple cloud on his skin;
He muttered that his wife would not approve.

I gilded his lung with pneumonia;
He complained to a physician.

I tinted his urine with blood;
He found this embellishment execrable.

So, I gave his eyes darkness until
He cried for the colours I'd taken away.

Vitreous China

My ribs begin to nag like teeth.

I want to sew my mouth with gut
and plait my lashes, staple nostrils,

wax and seal my ear-holes flush
and plug my pores and follicles

then cauterise my anus, wrap
my vulva up in masking tape.

Short-Love Couplets

i

When we are as joyous as African funeral music,
You will take me from behind with a loaded
 hypodermic.

ii

We kissed for love and to exchange
Your chancre for my gingivitis.

iii

The beauty at the heart of poison ~
Tensed between the tip and broken skin.

iv

The reality of hospital.
The memory of making love to your colostomy.

v

It: no longer floating in that amniotic swim
But waiting till the umbilical's slipped over the rim.

vi

My lymphocytes engaged but you:
A funeral cortège on blood road.

Viral

Beneath the epidermis is a battered endoderm,
The flesh gone to pulp.
There is as yet no outward sign of injury.

The brain is already dissected
(Though meninges are intact):
Dura matter, arachnoid, pia matter.

This cadaver has been scooped out
But its shell, when struck,
Will register none of the hollowness.

In Extremis: Lysergic Acid Diethylamide

i

Blinded, I reacted with relief.
Now, there was not light, but gravity
Impressing on the surfaces of eyeballs
That would no longer recognise me in reflection.

ii

A line became a circle
In behind my eyelids.
Soon it was a ripple
In the pool through which my body swam:
Corrosive liquid. Bone was all
And I, released from *functionfollowform*,
Was a compendium of marrow vessels
Drifting to the bottom:
The beginning of coral.

iii

And if my flesh and skin had stopped
Their slow recycling of the cells

And if my follicles had ceased
The foliation of the head

And if my fingernails were not allowed
To crawl out in an arc that would
In time impress a crescent
On each pad of fingertip

Sympathy

I missed out on your death
And had never come to see you
In the home where you had left
Your faculties at the door.

When the phone call came,
The sun was going down into the sill.
I lit up a roll-your-own,
Then e-mailed all my friends.

In the funeral parlour
I saw your yellow body.
Your white hair seemed applied,
Your skin unreal until I noticed
~ Close up ~ veins like circuitry.

Your lips had shrivelled back into the buccal cavity,
Terrified of herpes-bearing mourners
Here to cry over the coffin
In which you seemed pre-shrunk to fit.

I did not cry,
But checked your wrist for a pulse.

Sub Rosa

Watching a lover wash cutlery,
One glove concealing a lesion
On a hand that sails through water
Like a submarine of flesh:
The fingers, bony periscopes
That spy in wrong directions.

Robert Mapplethorpe:
Aspects of *Self-Portrait 1988*

Shutter Open

Left hand clutching the knee,
Attempting to reclaim
The patella from infection.

Right hand clenching in a relic gesture
Reminiscent of an infant sucking its thumb.

Time Lapse

The props in this photograph
Are already transforming.

The dressing gown becomes a coffin;
The large leather armchair, a fire.
The crown-embroidered slippers walk away.

Development

Soon after this self portrait
The world made its excuses and left,
Closing my eyelids behind it.